Finding Yourself

A Spiritual Journey through a Florida Garden

Written by William W. Maxwell
Photographed by John Moran

Dedicated to Jonathan A. Shaw
whose vision, spirituality and concern for humanity's future
was the inspiration for this book.

John Moran 1999

© 1999 Bok Tower Gardens, William W. Maxwell and John Moran. All rights reserved. Published by The Bok Tower Ga...
Printed and bound in the U.S.A. Distributed by Bok Tower Gardens, 1151 Tower Boulevard, Lake Wales, Flori...

D1377293

THIS SINGING TOWER
WITH ITS ADJACENT SANCTUARY
WAS DEDICATED
AND PRESENTED FOR VISITATION
TO THE AMERICAN PEOPLE
BY CALVIN COOLIDGE
PRESIDENT OF THE UNITED STATES
FEBRUARY THE FIRST
NINETEEN HUNDRED AND TWENTY NINE

Foreword

The text and photographs in this book were prepared by Bill Maxwell, a columnist for the *St. Petersburg Times*, and John Moran, senior photographer and a columnist for *The Gainesville Sun*.

Bill Maxwell is a frequent visitor to Bok Tower Gardens and his words, now set as free verse, appeared first as a column that received a warm and astonishing response from the readers of the *St. Petersburg Times*. His words express the universality of the garden experience as a metaphor for the harmony of man and nature, and John Moran's photographs expand that spiritual vision.

Their inspiration is Bok Tower Gardens, created by Edward Bok, editor of *The Ladies' Home Journal*, and author/philanthropist. He was born at Den Helder, Netherlands in 1863 and came to the United States when he was six years old. A success in the publishing field, he is best remembered for his Pulitzer Prize-winning autobiography, *The Americanization of Edward Bok*, published on the 50th anniversary of his arrival in the United States.

His greatest gift to the American people is the sanctuary for "birds and people" that he created, which is known today as Bok Tower Gardens. Inspired by his grandfather, who joined his friends in transforming a bleak desert island in the North Sea into a haven for birds, Bok chose the highest spot in central Florida, Iron Mountain, to build his sanctuary. The inspiration came, Edward Bok said, "of that stuff of which dreams are made" and fulfilled the words that he received from his grandmother as he embarked for America: "Make you the world a bit better or more beautiful because you have lived in it."

In 1922, Edward Bok asked America's most famous living landscape architect, Frederick Law Olmsted, Jr., to transform Iron Mountain from a sandy hill of pines and palmettos into a sanctuary that would "touch the soul with its beauty and quiet."

Edward Bok's vision of a sanctuary for "people and birds" reflected his love of nature, music and the fine arts. For nearly seventy years, Bok Tower Gardens has provided visitors a retreat of beauty, refuge and learning.

Jonathan A. Shaw
President, Bok Tower Gardens
Lake Wales, Florida (1983 – 1998)

𝒜 Note from the Author

My job as a columnist for the *St. Petersburg Times* is a pressure cooker, to use a cliche. Nearly every day, I, like my fellow journalists, work against a deadline while fielding telephone calls from angry readers, answering letters and e-mail messages and conducting research in preparation to write.

The newsroom is oppressive, its culture of competition and accuracy framing nearly everything we do and think. At least once a month, I must get out of here to rest my soul, to calm the conflicting forces and emotions that fill each moment. I come to Bok Tower Gardens, an oasis where I find solace and spiritual refreshment.

Sure, I could visit other places, but nowhere else compares with Bok. Nowhere else has its beauty and quietude, its power to heal, its ability to make me feel special. Here, I feel at rest and totally at home.

This poem, then, is a heartfelt expression of my love for Bok Tower Gardens, one of the most beautiful places on planet Earth.

William W. Maxwell
January 1998

Best Wishes,
Bill 1999

I feel a change

    even as I pull into the parking lot.

      I feel refreshed

deep down inside.

"Here," reads a plaque,

    "all living things are respected,

      all people are welcomed."

I walk only a few paces

        before the mixed fragrances

and bright colors of native plants

        and the songs

        of thousands of birds

        entice me

        into this paradise.

No matter which path I choose,

I will walk

beneath a canopy of live oaks

draped with Spanish moss.

If a gentle breeze blows,

the moss sways,

forming lazy semi-circles

in the light.

*O*n this day,

    I choose the North Walk,

On which I pass

    a giant crinum

    with its lily-like flowers.

Looking

    toward a patch of lantana

        at the base of a palm,

I see a butterfly flittering

    from petal to petal.

I stand there,

    intrigued that this tiny creature

    can fill me

    with such wonder.

I want to touch its beauty,

    to experience its freedom.

A mockingbird sings overhead,

      and two red-bellied woodpeckers

           dip toward a petrified pine

     framed against the sky.

a rabbit hops

within a few feet of me.

       A squirrel begs for food.

A spider's web,

    glistening silver and green,

hangs across two ferns.

    A hummingbird,

      like a friendly ghost,

    darts in and out of the shadows

    and alights

    on a blooming abelmoschus.

The winding path

    is trimmed on each side

      with thousands

    of camellias and azaleas.

As I pause

   to admire a flowering mussaenda

and a row of coleus,

my eyes are pulled

to the darkest clump of leaves

   of a bay tree.

The two big eyes there

   belong to

      a great horned owl.

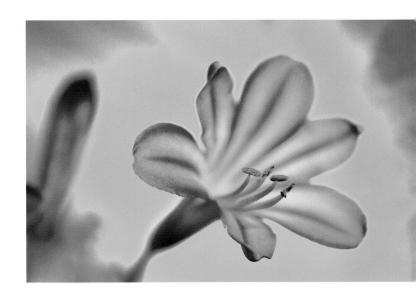

I wonder

   if anyone else knows

that it is there.

*W*ith my secret safe,

I follow a trail

that opens

into a bigger one.

Leaves crunch beneath my feet,

and the sounds echo

for a moment.

From here

      I can see the reflection pool

where two swans

      maneuver effortlessly

around a lily pad.

As they move

      in the direction

of the pink bell tower,

      I look to the sky.

Music fills the air.

The carillon is

as melodious as ever!

I feel as if

I were outside of my body.

I am at peace.

The adults around me

speak in hushed tones.

Even the youngest children

apprehend

that something special

is taking place.

An older couple stand

       near the bench

where I sit in the shade;

       the man's eyes are closed;

the woman stares

       at the goldfish in the pool

She embraces him.

The two of them rock

back and forth, letting the music

have its way.

I recall the comment,

"Not only

must the carillon be in tune,

the hearers

must be in tune

with the carillon."

From here,

I walk to the

Window by the Pond,

my favorite place.

A sign says it all:

"Be patient here.

This is nature's show

and it does not necessarily

match our schedules."

Window By The Pond

Sit awhile and relax. You may see a gallinule, alligator, green heron, water snake, wood duck or just a peaceful scene. This is Nature's Show, not ours. No scheduled performances.

On this day,

I see alligators,

egrets, ibises, kingfishers,

blackbirds,

thrushes, gallinules,

wood ducks,

blue-gray gnatcatchers.

On top of Iron Mountain,

I look down upon land

that was part of the ocean floor

half a million years ago.

The fossils of

prehistoric creatures –

dinosaurs,

mastodons,

tigers, camels and lions –

are buried

beneath centuries

of sawtooth palmetto,

wild grasses,

prickly pear cacti and scrub oak.

I am looking at humanity's past.

I feel small,

       yet significant at the same time.

I feel alive.

A breeze sweeps over me,

wafting heat

       and the fragrance of magnolia.

A dragonfly dances before me,

    pulling me

       out of my reverie.

Turning to depart,

I experience anew

the real secret of Bok Tower Gardens:

its quietude,

a spiritual presence

that induces

a feeling of contentment.

Again

    at the reflection pool,

        I stare at my image,

this time

    silhouetted

        by the late afternoon sun.

        A swan passes,

    sending symmetrical ripples

        across the dark water.

The infinite

expanse of the sky

shines in the pool,

endowing everything

with beauty.

I am part of it all.

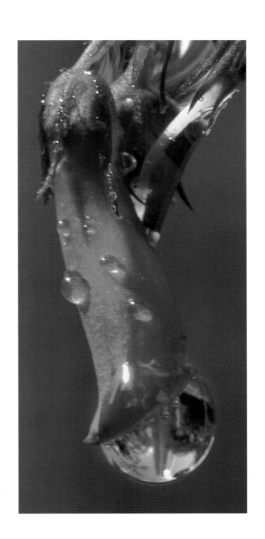

WILLIAM W. MAXWELL

William W. Maxwell is an editorial writer for the *St. Petersburg Times*. He joined the Times in 1994 after six years as a weekly columnist for *The Gainesville Sun* and *The New York Times Syndicate*. Prior to that, Maxwell was an investigative reporter for the *Fort Pierce Tribune*. He taught college English and journalism for 20 years before joining the *St. Petersburg Times*.

Maxwell has won many honors including, in 1989 and 1991, awards for general excellence in commentary by the Florida Press Club. He is a Fort Lauderdale, Florida native and a graduate of Bethune-Cookman College and the University of Chicago. He also attended the University of Florida Graduate School of Journalism.

Maxwell founded Role Models Foundation, Inc., in 1995, to encourage and inspire young people to build successful lives through the discipline of journalism.

JOHN MORAN

In wonder and gratitude, John Moran photographs the nature of Florida.

Moran is senior photographer and a columnist for *The Gainesville Sun*. A University of Florida journalism graduate, Moran's photography has appeared in numerous books and magazines, including *National Geographic, Life, Time, Newsweek, Smithsonian* and on the cover of the *National Audubon Society Field Guide to Florida*.

Moran has been named Photographer of the Year for the Southeastern U.S. by the National Press Photographers Association.

On photographing the nature of Florida, Moran says, "Truly a universal language, photography can help us better understand and appreciate the many gifts of nature bestowed upon this great state we call home."

ROLE MODELS FOUNDATION, INC.

Role Models Foundation, Inc. was created by William W. Maxwell in 1995.

At first, the sole purpose of Role Models Foundation, Inc. was to help young African Americans to succeed in their endeavors. However, as time passed and the idea gained support from the community, the program was expanded to include all youth, with emphasis on those who experience barriers.

The Foundation exists only to help youth develop their sense of self-worth and self-confidence through the discipline of journalism.

An online magazine, *Role Models Today*, is published by students for students in many cities in Florida. Several of the state's leading newspapers help with the printing and distribution of the paper.

Angela Clifford, Vice President of Role Models Foundation, deserves credit for recognizing that the column William Maxwell wrote about Bok Tower Gardens was indeed a poem.

A portion of the proceeds of the sale of this book will be donated to Role Models Foundation, Inc., Gainesville, Florida.